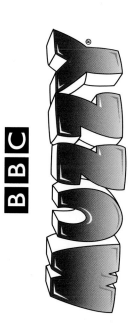

Original English Scripts:	Wendy Harris
	Joe Hambrook
	Richard Taylor
Spanish version:	Juan Antonio Ollero
German version:	Claudia Eilers
French version:	Elizabeth Gruninger
Italian version:	Arturo Tosi
Music:	Peter Shade
Animation:	Richard Taylor Cartoon Films Ltd.
Additional Animation:	Jollyfication Pty.
Graphic Designer:	Alfonso Lara
Executive Producer:	Joe Hambrook
Production Co-ordinator:	Amanda Loveday
DVD Authoring:	Ediciones Digitales, S.A.
Director:	Richard Taylor
Depósito Legal:	M-46361-2005

INDEX

BBC MUZZY

English	Español	Français	Deutsch	Italiano
King	Rey	Roi	König	Re
Queen	Reina	Reine	Königin	Regina
Muzzy	Muzzy	Muzzy	Muzzy	Muzzy
Corvax	Corvax	Corvax	Corvax	Corvax
Bob	Juan	Jean	Bob	Toni
Sylvia	Silvia	Sylvie	Sylvia	Silvia
Norman	Carlos	Albert	Norbert	Carlo
Amanda*	Amanda*	Amandine*	Amanda*	Amanda*
Thimbo*	Timbo*	Timbo*	Timbo*	Timbo*

(*) Muzzy II

ENGLISH

Level I. Part 1.

Part 1

Scene 1

King How do you do?
I'm the King.
I'm the King of Gondoland.

Queen How do you do?
I'm the Queen.

Sylvia Hello. I'm Princess Sylvia.
Bob Oh, Sylvia! Sylvia!

Bob Hello. I'm Bob.
I'm the gardener.

Corvax How do you do? I'm Corvax
King Thank you, Corvax.
Muzzy Hi! I'm Muzzy. Big Muzzy.
Norman Good Morning.
King Good Morning.

Scene 2

Song

Norman Good morning.
I'm Norman.
Good morning.
Good morning.
Good morning.
Good morning.
Good afternoon.
Good afternoon.
Good afternoon.
Good afternoon.

Good evening.
Good evening.
Good evening.

Good night.

Moon   Good night.
Sun   Good night.
Moon   Good night.

Scene 3

King   I'm strong.
Queen   I'm fat. I'm fat.
   I'm fat. I'm fat.

Sylvia   I'm beautiful.
Corvax   I'm clever.
Bob   I'm brave.
King   Strong.
Queen   Fat.
Sylvia   Beautiful

Corvax   Clever.
Bob   And brave.
Queen   You're strong.
King   Yes, I am. And you're fat.
Queen   Yes, I am.
Bob   And she's beautiful.

Corvax Yes, she is.
Sylvia He's brave.
  And he's clever.
Corvax No, no! I'm clever.
  I'm clever.
  Clever! Clever!
King Strong.
Queen Fat.
Sylvia Beautiful.
Corvax Clever.
Bob And brave.

Muzzy Big. I'm big. Big Muzzy.

Scene 4

Muzzy I'm big Muzzy.
Cat Big.
Muzzy Small.
Cat Big.
Muzzy Small.

King Big.
Bob Small.
  Big.
  Small.
Muzzy And I'm big Muzzy.

Scene 5

Sylvia I've got a bag. A big bag.
I've got a map.
I've got a hamburger.

Bob I've got a bike.
A motorbike.

Corvax I've got a computer.

King I've got a garden. Look!
I've got plums.
I've got peaches.
I've got grapes.

Queen I like plums. I like peaches.
I like grapes.

King And I like grapes.

Sylvia Hello, Mummy.*
Hello, Daddy.
Can I have a peach, please?

Scene 6

Norman I like hamburgers. Can I have
a hamburger, please?

Waiter Here you are.

---

* Mommy

Norman Thank you.
Can I have a salad, please?

Waiter Here you are.

Norman Thank you.
Can I have a drink, please?

Waiter Here you are.

Norman Thank you. Can I have an ice-cream, please?

Waiter Here you are.

Norman Thank you. Can I have a wash, please?*

Scene 7

Sylvia Can I have a peach please, Daddy?

King Yes. A peach!

Queen A peach.

Sylvia Thank you. Can I have a plum and some grapes, please?

King Yes. A plum and some grapes!

Queen A plum and some grapes.

Sylvia Thank you.

Scene 8

Cat A plum-a peach-a grape.
A plum-a peach-some grapes.
A plum-a plum-a plum!
Three plums! Jackpot!
Plums! Plums! Plums!

---

* Can I get cleaned up, please?

17

Scene 9

Corvax Bob!

Bob Yes?

Corvax Trees!

Bob Trees?

Corvax Yes. How many trees? Count!

Bob One, two, three, four, five, six, seven, eight, nine, ten.

Cat How many trees are there?

Computer One, two, three, four, five, six, seven, eight, nine, ten.

Corvax Bushes! How many bushes are there?

Bob There are two-four-six-eight-ten.

Corvax And how many flowers are there?

Bob Flowers?

Corvax Yes. Yes. How many flowers?

Bob A hundred? Two hundred? Three hundred? I don't know.

Scene 10

Norman I don't know.

Scene 11

Bob A hundred and seven. A hundred and eight.

Sylvia A hundred and nine.

Bob A hundred and ten.

Sylvia Bob! Can I have a rose, please?

Sylvia Thank you. I like roses.

Bob And I like you.

Sylvia Oh, look! I've got a rose. I've got a plum and a peach and some grapes. A hamburger and a map.

Bob And I've got... a bike. I love you.

Sylvia And I love you.

Bob/Sylvia Off we go!

Corvax No! No! No! I love the Princess! I love Sylvia!

Scene 12

Song

Bob/Sylvia A, E, I, O, U
I love you.
A, U, O, I, E
You love me.

Scene 13

King The gardener loves the Princess?

Corvax Yes! Yes!

King No! No! No!

Queen The Princess loves the gardener?

Corvax Yes! Yes!

Queen No! No!

King Come on!
Off we go!
Follow me!

All Bye!

A, E, I, U, O
Off we go.
I, O, U, E, A
Far, far away.

A, U, I, O, E
You love me.
A, E, I, O, U
I love you!
A, E, I, O, U
I love you!

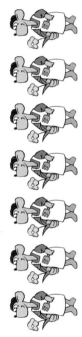

ESPAÑOL

Nivel I. Parte 1.

Parte 1

Escena 1

Rey
¿Cómo están ustedes?
Yo soy el Rey.
Soy el Rey de Gondolandia.
¿Cómo están ustedes?

Reina
Soy la Reina.

Silvia Hola. Soy la Princesa Silvia.
Juan ¡Oh, Silvia, Silvia!

Hola. Soy Juan.
Soy el jardinero.
¿Cómo están ustedes?

Corvax Soy Corvax.

Rey Gracias Corvax.
Muzzy Hola. Soy Muzzy.
Muzzy el Grande.

Carlos Buenos días.
Rey Buenos días.

Escena 2

Canción

Carlos Buenos días. Soy Carlos.
Buenos días.
Buenos días.
Buenos días.
Buenos…
Buenas tardes.
Buenas tardes.
Buenas tardes.

Reina Soy gorda. Soy gorda.
Soy gorda. Soy gorda.
Silvia Soy hermosa.
Corvax Soy listo.
Juan Soy valiente.
Rey Fuerte.
Reina Gorda.
Silvia Hermosa.

Corvax Listo.
Juan Valiente.
Reina Tú eres fuerte.
Rey Sí, yo lo soy. Y tú eres gorda.

Luna Buenas tardes.
Sol Buenas tardes.
Luna Buenas tardes.
Buenas tardes.
Buenas noches.
Buenas noches.
Buenas noches.
Buenas noches.

Escena 3

Rey Soy fuerte.

Reina	Sí, yo lo soy.
Juan	Y ella es hermosa.
Corvax	Sí, ella lo es.
Silvia	Él es valiente. Y él es listo.
Corvax	No, no. Yo soy listo.
	Yo soy listo. Listo. Listo.
Rey	Fuerte.
Reina	Gorda.
Silvia	Hermosa.
Corvax	Listo.
Juan	Valiente.

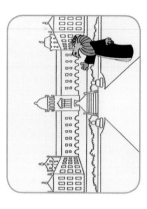

Muzzy	Y yo soy grande.
	Muzzy el Grande.

Muzzy	Soy Muzzy el Grande.
Gato	Grande.
Muzzy	Pequeño.
Gato	Grande.
Muzzy	Pequeño.

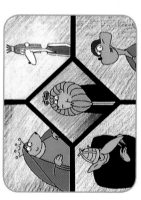

Rey	Grande.
Juan	Pequeña.
	Grande.
	Pequeño.
Muzzy	Y yo soy Muzzy el Grande.

Escena 5

Silvia
Tengo un bolso.
Un bolso grande.
Tengo un mapa.
Tengo una hamburguesa.

Juan
Tengo una moto.
Una motocicleta.

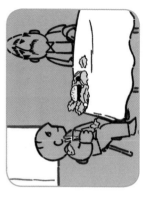

Corvax
Yo tengo un ordenador.

Rey
Tengo un jardín. Miren.
Tengo ciruelas. Tengo
melocotones. Tengo uvas.

Reina
Me gustan las ciruelas.
Me gustan los melocotones.
Me gustan las uvas.

Rey
Y a mí me gustan las uvas.

Silvia
Hola, mamá. Hola, papá.
¿Me puedes dar un
melocotón, por favor?

Escena 6

Carlos
Me gustan las hamburguesas.
¿Me puede dar una
hamburguesa, por favor?

Camarero	Aquí tiene.
Carlos	Gracias. ¿Me puede dar una ensalada, por favor?
Camarero	Aquí tiene.
Carlos	Gracias. ¿Me puede dar algo de beber, por favor?
Camarero	Aquí tiene.
Carlos	Gracias. ¿Me puede dar un helado, por favor?
Camarero	Aquí tiene.
Carlos	Gracias. ¿Me puede limpiar, por favor?

Escena 7

Silvia	¿Me puedes dar un melocotón, por favor?
Rey	Sí. Un melocotón.
Reina	Un melocotón.
Silvia	Gracias.
	¿Me puedes dar una ciruela y unas uvas, por favor?
Rey	Sí. Una ciruela y unas uvas.
Reina	Una ciruela y unas uvas.
Silvia	Gracias.

Escena 8

Gato	Una ciruela, un melocotón, una uva. Una ciruela, un melocotón, unas uvas. Una ciruela, una ciruela, una ciruela. Tres ciruelas. ¡Bingo! Ciruelas, ciruelas, ciruelas.

Escena 9

Juan ¿Sí?

Corvax ¡Árboles!

Juan ¿Árboles?

Corvax Sí. ¿Cuántos árboles? Cuéntalos.

Juan Uno, dos, tres, cuatro, cinco, seis, siete, ocho, nueve, diez.

Gato ¿Cuántos árboles hay?

Ordenador Uno, dos, tres, cuatro, cinco, seis, siete, ocho, nueve, diez.

Corvax Arbustos.

Juan ¿Cuántos arbustos hay?

Hay: dos, cuatro, seis, ocho, diez.

Corvax ¿Y cuántas flores hay?

Juan ¿Flores?

Corvax Sí, sí. ¿Cuántas flores?

Juan ¿Cien? ¿Doscientas? ¿Trescientas? No lo sé.

Escena 10

Carlos No lo sé.

Escena 11

Juan Ciento siete. Ciento ocho.

Silvia Ciento nueve.

Juan Ciento diez.

Silvia Juan. ¿Me puedes dar una rosa, por favor?

Silvia Gracias.

Yo quiero a Silvia.

Escena 12

Canción

Juan/Silvia A-E-I-O-U
te quiero.
A-U-O-I-E,
me quieres.
A-E-I-O-U,
vámonos.

Juan Me gustan las rosas.
Silvia Y a mí me gustas tú.
Mira. Tengo una rosa.
Tengo una ciruela y un
melocotón y unas uvas.
Tengo una hamburguesa y
un mapa.
Juan Y yo tengo una moto.
Te quiero.
Silvia Y yo te quiero a tí.
Ambos Vámonos.
Corvax No, no, no.
Yo quiero a la Princesa.

I-O-U-E-A,
vámonos ya.
A-U-I-O-E,
quiéreme.
A-E-I-O-U,
te quiero.
A-E-I-O-U,
¿me quieres tú?

Escena 13

Rey ¿El jardinero quiere a la Princesa?

Corvax Sí, Sí.

Rey No, no, no.

Reina ¿La Princesa quiere al jardinero?

Corvax Sí, sí.

Reina No, no, no.

Rey Venga, vámonos. Seguidme.

Todos Adiós.

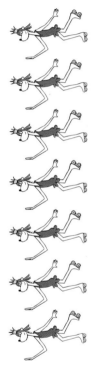

FRANÇAIS

Niveau I. Partie 1.

Partie 1

Scène 1

Roi Comment allez-vous ?
Je suis le Roi.
Je suis le Roi de Gondolie.

Reine Comment allez-vous ?
Je suis la Reine.

Sylvie Bonjour.
Je suis la Princesse Sylvie.

Jean Sylvie...Sylvie....
Bonjour. Je suis Jean.
Je suis le jardinier.
Comment allez-vous ?

Corvax Je suis Corvax.

Roi Merci, Corvax.

Muzzy Salut ! Je suis Muzzy.
Le Grand Muzzy.

Albert Bonjour.

Roi Bonjour.

Scène 2

Chanson

Albert Bonjour. Je suis Albert.
Bonjour.
Bonjour.
Bonjour.
Bonjour.
Bonjour.
Bonjour.

33

Scène 3

Roi Je suis fort.
Reine Je suis grosse. Je suis grosse. Je suis grosse. Je suis grosse. Je suis grosse.
Sylvie Je suis belle.

Corvax Je suis malin.
Jean Je suis courageux.
Roi Fort !
Reine Grosse !
Sylvie Belle !
Corvax Malin !

Bonjour.
Bonjour.
Bonsoir.
Bonsoir.
Bonsoir.
Bonne nuit.

Lune Bonne nuit.
Soleil Bonne nuit.
Lune Bonne nuit.

Jean	Courageux !
Reine	Tu es fort.
Roi	Oui, je suis fort.
	Et toi, tu es grosse.
Reine	Oui, je suis grosse.
Jean	Et elle, elle est belle.
Corvax	Oui, elle est belle.
Sylvie	Il est courageux.
	Et il est malin.

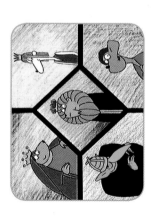

Corvax	Non, non ! Moi, je suis malin. Je suis malin. Malin ! Malin !

Roi	Fort !
Reine	Grosse !
Sylvie	Belle !
Corvax	Malin !
Jean	Courageux !
Muzzy	Et grand ! Et moi, je suis grand. Le Grand Muzzy.

Scène 4

Muzzy	Grand.
Chat	Petit.
Muzzy	Je suis le Grand Muzzy.

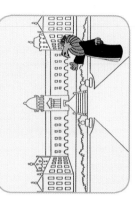

35

Chat	Grand.
Muzzy	Petit.
Chat	Grand.
Muzzy	Petit.
Roi	Grand.
Jean	Petit. Grand. Petit.
Muzzy	Et moi, je suis le Grand Muzzy.

Scène 5

Sylvie	Chut !... J'ai un sac.
	Un grand sac.
	J'ai une carte.
	J'ai un hamburger.
Jean	J'ai une moto.
	Une motocyclette !
Corvax	J'ai un ordinateur.
Roi	J'ai un jardin. Regardez. J'ai des prunes. J'ai des pêches.
	J'ai du raisin.
Reine	J'aime les prunes. J'aime les pêches. J'aime le raisin.

Roi	Et moi, j'aime le raisin.
Sylvie	Salut, maman ! Salut, papa !... Tu peux me donner une pêche, s'il te plaît?

Scène 6

Albert	J'aime les hamburgers. Vous pouvez me donner un hamburger, s'il vous plaît ?
Serveur	Et voilà !
Albert	Merci. Vous pouvez me donner une salade, s'il vous plaît ?

Sylvie Tu peux me donner une pêche, s'il te plaît, papa ?

Roi Oui, une pêche !

Reine Une pêche.

Sylvie Merci. Tu peux me donner une prune et du raisin, s'il te plaît ?

Roi Oui. Une prune et du raisin !

Reine Une prune et du raisin.

Sylvie Merci.

Serveur Et voilà !

Albert Merci. Vous pouvez me donner une boisson, s'il vous plaît ?

Serveur Et voilà !

Albert Merci. Vous pouvez me donner une glace, s'il vous plaît ?

Serveur Et voilà !

Albert Merci. Vous pouvez me donner une douche, s'il vous plaît ?

Scène 8

Chat Miaou ! Une prune, une
pêche, du raisin.
Une prune, une pêche, du
raisin. Une prune, une prune,
une prune !
Trois prunes ! Gagné !
Des prunes ! Des prunes !!
Des prunes !!!

Scène 9

Corvax Jean !

Jean Oui ?

Corvax Arbres.

Jean Arbres ?

Corvax Oui. Combien y a-t-il d'arbres?
Compte-les !

Jean Un, deux, trois, quatre, cinq,
six, sept, huit, neuf, dix.

Chat Combien d'arbres y a-t-il ?

Ordinateur Un, deux, trois, quatre, cinq,
six, sept, huit, neuf, dix.

Corvax Buissons. Combien y a-t-il de
buissons ?

Jean Il y en a... deux... quatre...
six... huit... dix.

Corvax Et combien de fleurs y a-t-il ?

Jean Des fleurs ?

Corvax Oui, oui ! Combien de fleurs ?

Jean Cent ? Deux cents ? Trois
cents ?
Je ne sais pas.

Scène 10

Albert Je ne sais pas.

Scène 11

Jean Cent sept, cent huit...
Sylvie Et cent neuf...
Jean Et cent dix...

Sylvie Jean ! Tu peux me donner une rose ? S'il te plaît ?... Merci. J'aime les roses.

Jean Et moi, je t'aime.
Sylvie Regarde. J'ai une rose. J'ai une prune et une pêche et du raisin.
Sylvie Un hamburger et une carte.
Jean Et moi, j'ai...une moto. Je t'aime.
Sylvie Moi, aussi, je t'aime.
Jean/Sylv. On y va ?
Corvax Non, non, non, non !... Moi, j'aime la Princesse ! Moi, j'aime Sylvie !

Scène 12

Chanson

Jean/Sylv. A-e-i-o-u
Je t'aime.
A-u-o-i-e
Tu m'aimes.
A-e-i-u-o

En moto.
I-o-u-e-a
On y va.
A-u-i-o-e
Tous les deux.
A-e-i-o-u
Je t'aime.
A-e-i-o-u
M'aimes-tu ?

Scène 13

Roi — Le jardinier aime la Princesse ?

Corvax — Oui ! Oui !

Roi — Non ! Non ! Non !

Reine — La Princesse aime le jardinier ?

Corvax — Oui ! Oui !

Reine — Non ! Non ! Non !

Roi — Allez...On y va...Allons-y !

Tous — Au revoir !

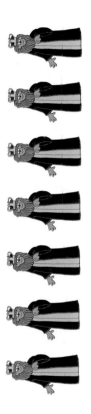

DEUTSCH

Stufe I. Teil 1.

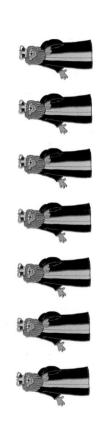

Szene 1

König Guten Tag. Ich bin der König.
Ich bin der König von Gondoland.

Königin Guten Tag. Ich bin die Königin.

Sylvia Hallo! Huiii... Ich bin Prinzessin Sylvia.

Bob Ach, Sylvia, Sylvia, Sylvia...
Hallo. Ich bin Bob.
Ich bin der Gärtner.

Corvax Guten Tag. Ich bin Corvax.
König Danke, Corvax.
Muzzy Hallo! Ich bin Muzzy.
Der große Muzzy!

Norbert Guten Morgen.
König Guten Morgen.

Szene 2

Lied

Norbert Guten Morgen.
Ich bin Norbert.
Guten Morgen.
Guten Morgen.
Guten Morgen.
Guten Morgen.
Guten... Tag.
Guten Tag.

König	Ich bin stark.
Königin	Ich bin dick. Ich bin dick.
Sylvia	Ich bin dick.
Corvax	Ich bin schön.
Bob	Ich bin klug.
König	Ich bin mutig.
Königin	Stark.
Sylvia	Dick.
Corvax	Schön.
Bob	Klug.
	Und mutig!

	Guten Tag.
	Guten Tag.
	Guten Tag.
	Guten Abend.
	Guten Abend.
	Guten Abend.
	Gute Nacht.
	Gute Nacht.
	Gute Nacht.
	Gute Nacht.
Mond	
Sonne	
Mond	

Königin Du bist stark.
König Ja, das stimmt.
Königin Und du bist dick.
König Ja, das stimmt.

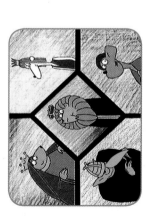

Bob Und sie ist schön.
Corvax Ja, das stimmt.
Sylvia Er ist mutig, und er ist klug.
Corvax Nein! Nein! Ich bin klug! Ich bin klug! Klug! Klug!
König Stark!
Königin Dick!
Sylvia Schön!

Corvax Klug!
Bob Und mutig!
Muzzy Groß! Ich bin groß! Der große Muzzy!

Szene 4

Muzzy Ich bin der große Muzzy.
Katze Groß.
Muzzy Klein.
Katze Groß.
Muzzy Klein.
König Groß.

Bob Klein. Groß. Klein.
Muzzy Und ich bin der große Muzzy.

Szene 5

Sylvia Psst! Ich habe eine Tasche. Eine große Tasche. Ich habe eine Karte. Ich habe einen Hamburger.
Bob Ich habe ein Rad. Ein Motorrad.
Corvax Ich habe einen Computer.

König Ich habe einen Garten. Seht! Ich habe Pflaumen. Ich habe Pfirsiche. Ich habe Trauben.
Königin Ich mag Pflaumen! Ich mag Pfirsiche. Ich mag Weintrauben!
König Ich mag auch Trauben.
Sylvia Hallo, Mutti. Hallo, Vati. Kann ich bitte einen Pfirsich haben?

Szene 6

Norbert Ich mag Hamburger. Kann ich bitte einen Hamburger haben?
Ober Hier, bitte.
Norbert Danke. Kann ich bitte einen Salat haben?
Ober Hier, bitte.
Norbert Danke. Kann ich bitte etwas zu trinken haben?

Ober   Hier, bitte.
Norbert   Danke. Kann ich bitte etwas Eis haben?
Ober   Hier, bitte.
Norbert   Danke. Kann ich bitte etwas Wasser haben?

Szene 7

Sylvia   Kann ich bitte einen Pfirsich haben, Vati?
König   Bitte. Einen Pfirsich.
Königin   Einen Pfirsich.

Sylvia   Danke. Kann ich bitte eine Pflaume und Weintrauben haben?

König   Bitte. Eine Pflaume und Weintrauben.
Königin   Eine Pflaume und Weintrauben.
Sylvia   Danke.

Szene 8

Katze   Eine Pflaume - ein Pfirsich -

eine Weintraube.
Eine Pflaume - ein Pfirsich -
Weintrauben.
Eine Pflaume - eine Pflaume
- eine Pflaume!
Drei Pflaumen! Hurra! Miau!
Pflaumen! Pflaumen!
Pflaumen!

Szene 9

Corvax   Bob!
Bob   Ja?

Corvax   Bäume!
Bob   Bäume?
Corvax   Ja! Wie viele Bäume sind
das? Zähl sie!
Bob   Eins, zwei, drei, vier,
fünf, sechs, sieben, acht,
neun, zehn.
Katze   Wie viele Bäume sind das?
Computer   Eins, zwei, drei, vier,
fünf, sechs, sieben,
acht, neun, zehn.
Corvax   Büsche! Wie viele Büsche
sind das?
Bob   Das sind... zwei - vier - sechs
- acht - zehn.
Corvax   Und wie viele Blumen
sind das?
Bob   Blumen?
Corvax   Ja! Ja! Wie viele Blumen?
Bob   Hundert? Zweihundert?
Dreihundert?
Ich weiß es nicht.

Szene 10

Norbert Ich weiß es nicht.

Szene 11

Bob Hundertsieben. Hundertacht.
Sylvia Hundertneun.
Bob Hundertzehn.
Sylvia Bob! - Kann ich eine Rose haben - bitte?
Bob Danke. Ich mag Rosen. Und ich mag dich.

Sylvia Sieh mal! Ich habe eine Rose. Ich habe eine Pflaume, einen Pfirsich und Weintrauben.
Sylvia Einen Hamburger und eine Karte.
Bob Und ich habe... ein Motorrad! Ich liebe dich!
Sylvia Und ich liebe dich.
Bob/Sylvia Los geht's!
Corvax Nein! Nein! Nein! Ich liebe die Prinzessin! Ich liebe Sylvia!

Szene 12

Lied

Bob/Sylvia A - E - I - O - U. Ich lieb' dich! A - U - O - I - E. Du liebst mich! A - E - I - U - O.

Wir fahren fort.
I - O - U - E - A.
Weit, weit fort.
A - U - I - O - E.
Wir sind allein.

A - E - I - O - U.
Du bist mein.
A - E - I - O - U.
Ich und du.

Szene 13

König   Der Gärtner liebt die Prinzessin?

Corvax   Ja! Ja!

König   Nein! Nein! Nein!!!

Königin   Die Prinzessin liebt den Gärtner?

Corvax   Ja! Ja!

Königin   Nein! Nein!

König   Kommt! Los geht's! Mir nach!

Alle   Bis bald!

ITALIANO

Livello I. Parte 1.

Parte 1

Scena 1

Re
Buongiorno
Io sono il Re.
Sono il Re di Gondolandia

Regina
Buongiorno.
Io sono la Regina

Silvia
Ciao! Io sono la Principessa
Silvia.

Toni
Oh, Silvia! Silvia!
Ciao! Io sono Toni.
Sono il giardiniere

Corvax
Buongiorno. Io sono Corvax

Re
Grazie, Corvax

Muzzy
Ciao! Io sono Muzzy.
Il grande Muzzy

Carlo
Buongiorno

Re
Buongiorno

Scena 2

Canzone

Carlo
Buongiorno. Sono Carlo.
Buongiorno.
Buongiorno.
Buongiorno.
Buongiorno.
Buongiorno.
Buongiorno.
Buongiorno.

Buongiorno.
Buonasera.
Buonasera.
Buonasera.
Buonanotte.

Luna Buonanotte.
Sole Buonanotte.
Luna Buonanotte.

Scena 3

Re Sono forte.

Regina Sono grassa. Sono grassa!
Sono grassa! Sono grassa!!
Silvia Io sono bella.
Corvax Io sono intelligente.
Toni Io sono coraggioso.
Re Forte.
Regina Grassa.
Silvia Bella.

Corvax Intelligente.
Toni E coraggioso.
Regina Tu sei forte.
Re Sì, lo sono. E tu sei grassa.

Regina Sì, lo sono.
Toni E lei è bella.
Corvax Sì, è bella.
Silvia Lui è coraggioso.
E intelligente.

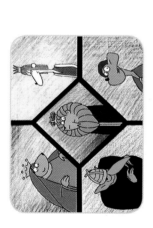

Corvax No, no, no! Io sono
intelligente. Io sono
intelligente. Intelligente.
Intelligente!
Re Forte!
Regina Grassa!
Silvia Bella

Corvax Intelligente!
Toni Coraggioso!
Muzzy E grande. E io sono grande.
Il Grande Muzzy.

Scena 4

Muzzy Sono il Grande Muzzy
Gatto Grande
Muzzy Piccolo
Gatto Grande.
Muzzy Piccola.
Re Grande.

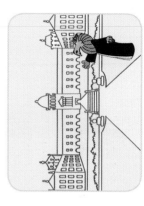

Toni Piccola. Grande. Piccola.
Muzzy E io sono il Grande Muzzy.

Scena 5

Silvia Sshh! Ho una borsa.
Una borsa grande.
Ho una mappa.
Ho un hamburger.
Toni Io ho una moto.
Una motocicletta.
Corvax Io ho un computer

Re Io ho un giardino. Guardate.
Ho delle susine. Ho delle pesche. Ho un po' d'uva.
Regina Mi piacciono le susine.
Mi piacciono le pesche.
Mi piace l'uva.
Re Anche a me piace l'uva.
Silvia Buongiorno mamma.
Buongiorno papà.
Posso prendere una pesca, per favore?

Scena 6

Carlo Mi piacciono gli hamburger.
Un hamburger, per favore.
Cameriere Eccolo
Carlo Grazie.
Un'insalata, per favore.
Cameriere Eccola.
Carlo Grazie.
Una bibita, per favore.

Cameriere Eccola.
Carlo Grazie.
Un gelato, per favore.
Cameriere Eccolo.
Carlo Grazie.
E una doccia, per favore.

Scena 7

Silvia Posso prendere una pesca, per favore?
Re Si. Una pesca!
Regina Una pesca.

Silvia Grazie. Posso prendere una susina e un po' d'uva, per favore?

Re Si. Una susina e un po' d'uva.
Regina Una susina e un po' d'uva.
Silvia Grazie.

Scena 8

Gatto Miao! Una susina, una pesca, un chicco d'uva.

Una susina, una pesca, un grappolo d'uva.
Una susina, una susina, una susina. Tre susine! Tombola! Susine, susine, susine!

Scena 9

Corvax Toni!
Toni Sì?

Corvax Alberi!
Toni Alberi?

Corvax Sì. Quanti alberi? Contali!
Toni Uno, due, tre, quattro, cinque, sei, sette, otto, nove, dieci.
Gatto Quanti alberi ci sono?
Computer Uno, due, tre, quattro, cinque, sei, sette, otto, nove, dieci.
Corvax Cespugli! Quanti cespugli ci sono?
Toni Ce ne sono due, quattro, sei, otto, dieci
Corvax E quanti fiori ci sono?
Toni Fiori?
Corvax Sì. Sì. Quanti fiori?
Toni Cento? Duecento? Trecento? Non lo so.

Scena 10

Carlo Eh! Non lo so.

Scena 11

Toni Centosette. Centootto.
Silvia Centonove.
Toni Centodieci.
Silvia Toni. Mi dai una rosa, per favore?

Silvia Grazie. Mi piacciono le rose.
Toni E a me piaci tu.
Silvia Oh, guarda! Ho una rosa. Ho una susina e una pesca e un po' d'uva.

Silvia Ho un hamburger e una mappa.
Toni E io ho...una moto. Ti amo.
Silvia Anch'io ti amo.
Toni/Silvia Andiamo!
Corvax No, no, no! Io amo la principessa. Io amo Silvia.

Scena 12

Canzone

Bob/Silvia A, E, I, O, U.
Ti amo.
A, U, O, I, E.
Amore.
A, E, I, U, O.
Andiamo.
I, O, U, E, A.
Via via di qua.
A, U, I, O, E.

Ami me?
A, E, I, O, U.
Ti amo!

A, E, I, O, U.
Sempre più.

Scena 13

Re   Il giardiniere ama la Principessa?

Corvax   Sì. Sì

Re   No! No! No!

Regina   La Principessa ama il giardiniere?

Corvax   Sì. Sì

Regina   No! No!

Re   Venite! Andiamo! Seguitemi!

Tutti   Arrivederci!